The NatureTrail Book of
SEASHORE LIFE

Su Swallow

Identifying Seashore Animals and Plants with this book

This book is about common birds, shells, seaweeds, flowers, fish, crabs and other creatures you can find on the seashore. When you find or see something, and you want to know what it is, use this book as follows:

Turn to the pages which deal with the **kind of animal or plant** you have seen. For example, pages 24–25 tell you about fish. If you can't see a picture of it there . . .

. . . turn to the back of the book (pages 28–31) and look it up in the section called **More Seashore Life to Spot,** where you may be able to find a picture of it.

If you still can't find it, look on other pages of the book, such as pages 4–5, which show you some of the hidden life on the beach. Always make careful notes about things you see, and try to identify them later.

First published in 1976 by
Usborne Publishing Ltd,
20 Garrick Street,
London WC2

Text and Artwork © 1976 by
Usborne Publishing Ltd.

Gannet

Puffin

Written by
Su Swallow

Series Editor
Sue Jacquemier

Consultant Editor
Jonathan Elphick

Special advice by
Staff of the Zoology and
Botany Departments of the
Natural History Museum,
London

Designed by
Sally Burrough

Illustrated by
David Baxter, Roland Berry,
Hilary Burn, Terry Callcut,
Victoria Gordon, Bob Hersey,
Colin King, Deborah King,
Patricia Mynott, David Nash,
Gill Platt, George Thompson,
Peter Warner, Phil Weare

Printed in Belgium

**Snakelocks ↑
Anemone**

Limpet

**Bladder
Wrack**

**Devil or
Fiddler Crab**

**Common
Starfish**

The NatureTrail Book of
SEASHORE LIFE

This book tells you where to look for common animals, birds, fish and plants on European coasts. It shows you lots of clues to look for, how animals and plants live in different kinds of places, and how to take notes and make collections. If you want to identify something you have found on the seashore, follow the instructions on page 1.

If you have enjoyed this book, you may want to look at some field guides. There is a list on page 32, as well as a list of clubs you can join.

Contents

Periwinkles

Common Mussel

Pelican's Foot Shell

Pod Razor Shell

Painted Top Shell

Queen Scallop

3

Hidden Life on the Beach . . .

This man may think he is alone on the beach, but in fact there are living creatures all around him. They have chosen places where they are difficult to spot, and where they are least likely to be disturbed by men or other animals. The numbers show you where six of them are hidden.

1

Sand-Eels often bury themselves in wet sand when the tide goes out. Look for them near the surf line. They will come to the surface if the sand near them is disturbed.

Sand-Eel

2

Common Starfish

Starfish usually live in the sea. If they get stranded on shore, they take shelter in pools of sea water among rocks. This one is opening a Scallop to eat it.

3

Herring Gull

Gulls always nest in places that are difficult for animals to get to. They usually choose ledges on cliffs. Watch out for birds flying to or from the nests.

...and How to Find it

Goose Barnacles

Goose Barnacles grow on stalks that look like the necks of geese. These were washed ashore on driftwood. They gather food with their fringe of tentacles.

Shore Crab

This Shore Crab is hiding in a clump of seaweed in a rock pool. Use a net to hunt for crabs, and put them back in sea water when you have finished with them.

What to Take

Fishing net

Magnifying glass

Trowel

Penknife

Notebook and pencil

Spade

Plastic screw-top containers

Bucket

Sieve

You will stand a better chance of finding the things that live on the beach if you take the right equipment with you. Whenever you make a discovery, note down the time and what part of the beach you were on. Wear what you want, but put on shoes or boots for wading in rock pools, so that you don't cut your feet.

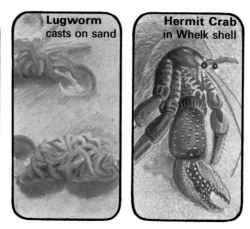

Lugworm casts on sand

Hermit Crab in Whelk shell

Prawn

Sea Anemone

Barnacles under a rock

Periwinkles on seaweed

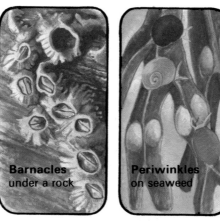

Sea Anemones are flesh-eating animals that look like plants. They live on small fish and shellfish, like this prawn. Their tentacles can sting.

The best time for exploring the beach is when the tide is furthest out. Check the local newspaper for the times of tides. Look on rocks for Barnacles and Limpets; in seaweed for Periwinkles and shellfish; under marks on wet sand for burrowing animals; and in empty shells for Hermit Crabs.

Exploring the Seashore

The kinds of animals and plants you find on the seashore will depend very much on the kind of beach you are exploring. Rocky, sandy and muddy beaches are good places to look. Shingle, or pebble, beaches are usually rather bare because the pebbles keep shifting, and at low tide they are too dry to support life. If you visit different kinds of beaches close together, notice how the creatures you find change from one beach to another. See which has more seaweeds, or more shells, where you find birds feeding, and so on.

Tides and Zones

The sea creeps up the shore, and then down again, roughly twice every 24 hours. These movements of the sea are called tides. The tides in the Mediterranean Sea are very small, and hard to notice, while the tides in other seas, like the Atlantic, are more obvious.

The highest point on the shore reached by the water is called "high water", and the lowest is called "low water". Spring tides (nothing to do with the season) happen roughly once a fortnight. They rise higher and fall lower than neap tides, which occur in between each spring tide.

The seashore can be divided into zones between the different high and low water levels. The picture below shows you the common seaweeds and shells that live in each zone.

HIGH WATER Spring tides

Small Periwinkles in rock crevice

Channel Wrack

Lichens

HIGH WATER Neap tides

Thick Top Shell

Rough Periwinkle on rock

Spiral Wrack

Flat Top Shell

Knotted Wrack

Splash Zone
A few animals and plants live here. They are sprayed, but not covered, by water.

Upper Zone
This zone is uncovered for days at a time. Fewer creatures live here than in the middle zone.

Middle Zone
This is the largest zone. Here you will find a wide variety of animals and seaweeds in large numbers.

1 Types of Coastline— Rocky Shores

Purple Sandpiper

Ravens

Groynes

The movement of the sea changes the shape of rocky shores. The water wears cliffs away and pulls pieces of rock down the shore, leaving the heaviest at the top. Groynes stop the rocks being swept too far *along* the shore.

2 Sand Dunes

Ringed Plover

WIND

Grasses are often planted on dunes to help stop the sand being blown further inland. If you would like to help with planting, contact the Nature Conservancy Council.

The Mediterranean Coast

Mediterranean Gulls

Blue Rock Thrush

You can sometimes see the tide mark on rocks in the Mediterranean.

↳ 60 cm. ↕

The seashore on the Mediterranean Sea has all the zones shown on this page, but they are telescoped into a very narrow band. The tide in the Mediterranean never rises and falls more than about 60 cm., so it is difficult to see the different zones. You will still be able, however, to find many of the plants and animals shown in this book. Look, too, for animals that can live more or less out of water, such as Land Crabs.

LOW WATER Neap tides

LOW WATER Spring tides

Sea

Bladder Wrack

Saw Wrack

Grey Top Shell

Painted Top Shell

Oarweeds

Common Periwinkle

Flat Periwinkle on seaweed

Lower Zone

This zone is only uncovered by the spring tides. Animals are less exposed to danger and so may be found in large numbers.

Shallow Water Zone

Plants and animals in this zone are always submerged, but as the water is shallow, its temperature varies.

3 Dykes

Brent Geese

Very flat coasts may be flooded by the sea. Dykes are built to hold back the water. A lot of wildlife may be found on these sheltered coasts.

Make your own Map of the Beach

String

WOOTTON BAY 2ND MAY 1976 LOW TIDE

3m. Splash Zone — Brown seaweed + Periwinkles

7m. Upper Zone — Thick Top Shell →

15m. Middle Zone — Knotted Wrack

10m. Lower Zone — Grey Top Shell →

Stretch a piece of string, tied to rocks at both ends, down the beach, and mark on your map everything that you see near the line. See if you can work out, from the seaweeds and shells you find, where the different zones begin and end. Make your map at low tide.

Seaweeds and their Secrets

You can find many kinds of seaweed growing on the shore, especially on rocky shores, and large deep-water seaweeds are often washed up after a storm. Compare them with land plants to see how well they are suited to life in the sea. Instead of growing roots, they anchor themselves to rocks or stones against the action of the waves. They take in food from the water, not the ground. Some can live both in and out of water as the tide goes in and out.

Check: some seaweeds have a thick vein, or **midrib**, running up the frond.

Check: what colour are the leaf-like branches (called **fronds**)? Are they flat or wavy, or broken along the edges?

Check: how long is the stalk, or **stipe**?

Holdfast. Check: is it disk-shaped or branched?

Brown Seaweed

Bladder wrack is one of the most common brown seaweeds. Use the check points in the picture to help you identify other seaweeds.

Some seaweeds have **air bladders**. They help to keep the plant upright in the water. Check: are they growing singly or in pairs?

Check: do fronds divide, or **branch**, or do they grow straight up from the holdfast? You can work out roughly how old Bladder Wrack is by counting two branchings for each year.

Bladder Wrack

1 At low tide seaweed growing on the shore lies flat.

2 At high tide the water holds it up.

Red Seaweed

Most red seaweeds are smaller than brown seaweeds. Look for them on rocks and in deep rock pools on the lower zone. Some feel hard and brittle, and look like coral.

Green Seaweed

Most green seaweeds are small, but they often grow in large clumps and cover rocks like a carpet. Look for them under large brown seaweeds on the upper and middle zones.

How Many Frond Shapes Can You Find?

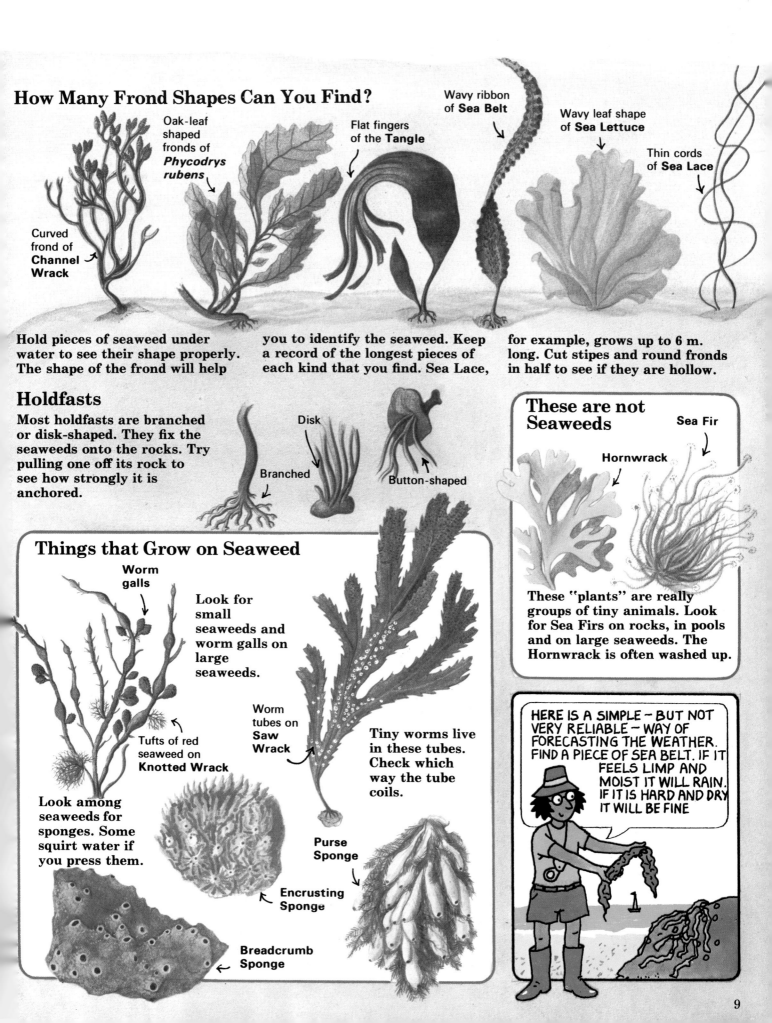

Oak-leaf shaped fronds of **Phycodrys rubens**

Flat fingers of the **Tangle**

Wavy ribbon of **Sea Belt**

Wavy leaf shape of **Sea Lettuce**

Thin cords of **Sea Lace**

Curved frond of **Channel Wrack**

Hold pieces of seaweed under water to see their shape properly. The shape of the frond will help you to identify the seaweed. Keep a record of the longest pieces of each kind that you find. Sea Lace, for example, grows up to 6 m. long. Cut stipes and round fronds in half to see if they are hollow.

Holdfasts

Most holdfasts are branched or disk-shaped. They fix the seaweeds onto the rocks. Try pulling one off its rock to see how strongly it is anchored.

Branched

Disk

Button-shaped

These are not Seaweeds

Sea Fir

Hornwrack

These "plants" are really groups of tiny animals. Look for Sea Firs on rocks, in pools and on large seaweeds. The Hornwrack is often washed up.

Things that Grow on Seaweed

Worm galls

Look for small seaweeds and worm galls on large seaweeds.

Tufts of red seaweed on **Knotted Wrack**

Worm tubes on **Saw Wrack**

Tiny worms live in these tubes. Check which way the tube coils.

Look among seaweeds for sponges. Some squirt water if you press them.

Purse Sponge

Encrusting Sponge

Breadcrumb Sponge

HERE IS A SIMPLE – BUT NOT VERY RELIABLE – WAY OF FORECASTING THE WEATHER. FIND A PIECE OF SEA BELT. IF IT FEELS LIMP AND MOIST IT WILL RAIN. IF IT IS HARD AND DRY IT WILL BE FINE

Rock Pools

A beach with rock pools can be one of the most exciting to explore. Here you will find animals that cannot survive out of water when the tide is out, as well as animals and plants that also live elsewhere on the shore. Look especially in pools with seaweed, which protects the animals from the sun and keeps the water temperature more even. Wear shoes that will not slip on wet rocks.

On windy days, when the surface of the rock pool is disturbed, look through the bottom of a clear plastic box to see into the pool. Keep very still and wait for animals to come out of hiding.

ALWAYS put rocks back the right way up to protect the animals living underneath.

Sea Anemones

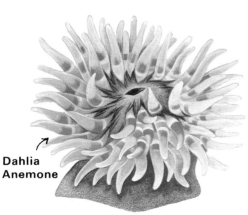

Dahlia Anemone

Sea anemones are animals. This one is usually camouflaged with bits of shell and gravel. If you prod it, it squirts water and contracts.

How a Beadlet Anemone Eats

1 **2** **3**

Tentacles drawn in

The **Beadlet Anemone** has 196 tentacles.

When the Beadlet Anemone is under water (see above), it waves its tentacles about in search of small fish or shrimps to eat (1). When one tentacle touches a fish, it stings it and the others close in (2) and push the fish into its mouth (3). When it is out of water it looks like a blob of jelly.

Shore Crab

The Shore Crab is common on the middle and lower zones. A crab carries its tail under its body. Check how many joints it has. Some also hide their fourth pair of legs.

Spider Crab

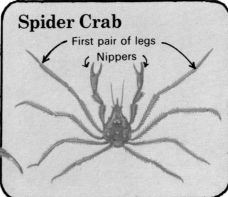

First pair of legs
Nippers

Look under stones and among seaweed on the lower zone for this crab. Its shell is about 1 cm. across. Notice the length of the first pair of legs.

Sea Urchin

The Sea Urchin's spines drop off when it dies. Some live on rocks and have a strong round shell. Other types burrow in the sand and have a more delicate, oval shell.

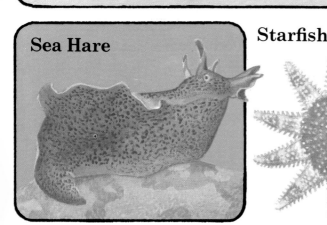

Lift aside thick clumps of seaweed to find the animals sheltering underneath.

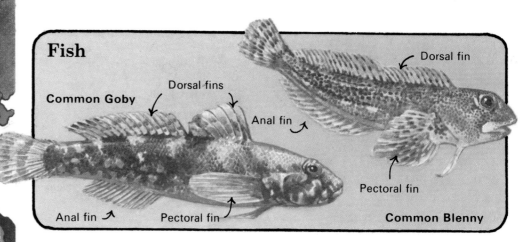

Fish

Common Goby — Dorsal fins — Anal fin

Dorsal fin

Pectoral fin

Common Blenny

Anal fin ⌐ — Pectoral fin

Blennies and Gobies are common in pools. Look at the fins to tell them apart. The Blenny has one long dorsal fin (the Goby has two), its anal fin is nearer the tail than the Goby's, and it has spiky pectoral fins (the Goby's are smoother and longer.)

Shrimps and Prawns

Shrimps and prawns are hard to spot because of their pale colours. Use a net to catch them. Prawns are larger (up to 15 cm.) than shrimps (up to 5 cm.) with feelers longer than their bodies.

Common Prawn

Common Shrimp

Brittle Stars

Look in pools among Coralline seaweeds for Brittle Stars. Handle them gently as their long thin arms break off easily.

Sea Hare

This Sea Hare has its shell in its body. It changes colour with age, from red to brown, then dark green. In summer, look for strings of its orange spawn round Oarweeds.

Starfish

Common Starfish

Common Sunstar

Cushion Star

Most starfish have five arms, but the Common Sunstar has up to 13. Look on the lower zone.

Look through a lens to see the rows of tube-feet (suckers) which pull the starfish along. Look in shallow shaded pools for the short-armed Cushion Star.

11

Flowers and Grasses

Many plants that grow by the sea are also found inland, but the seashore plants have to protect themselves against the salt spray and strong winds. Look at the leaves, the roots and the shape of the plants to see the differences. Some flowers can grow on any beach—even on shingle. Make a note of where you find flowers, and see if you can find the same flower on a different kind of beach.

Hawthorn is one of the few trees that grows by the sea. The wind dries out the soil on one side of the tree, so that its roots and branches only develop on the side away from the wind. They look as though they are being swept away.

Dunes

The picture shows how plants help to form dunes. The grasses have very long roots which hold down the sand in ridges, and stop the wind blowing the sand away. Marram grass is the most common.

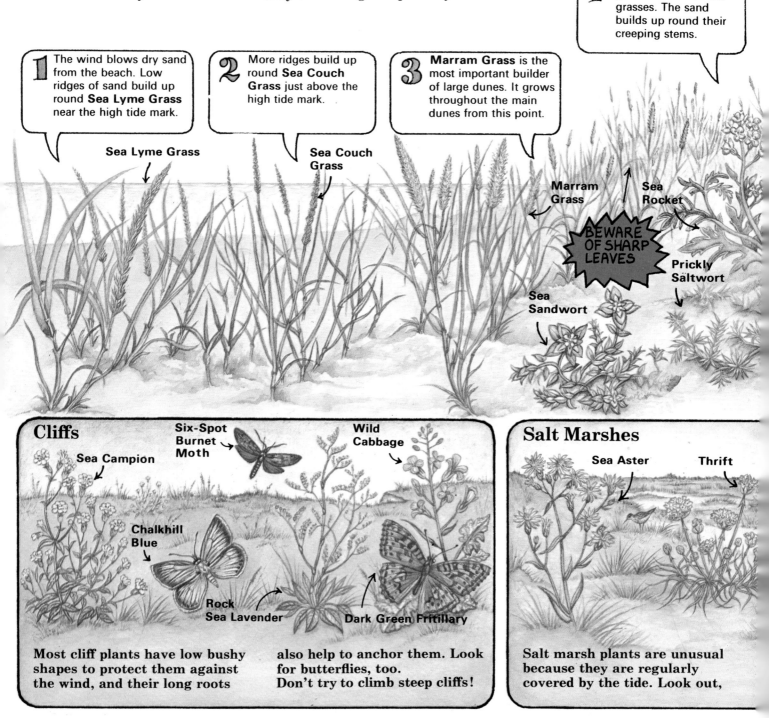

1 The wind blows dry sand from the beach. Low ridges of sand build up round **Sea Lyme Grass** near the high tide mark.

2 More ridges build up round **Sea Couch Grass** just above the high tide mark.

3 **Marram Grass** is the most important builder of large dunes. It grows throughout the main dunes from this point.

4 Small plants begin to grow in between the grasses. The sand builds up round their creeping stems.

Sea Lyme Grass

Sea Couch Grass

Marram Grass

Sea Rocket

BEWARE OF SHARP LEAVES

Prickly Saltwort

Sea Sandwort

Cliffs

Sea Campion

Six-Spot Burnet Moth

Wild Cabbage

Chalkhill Blue

Rock Sea Lavender

Dark Green Fritillary

Most cliff plants have low bushy shapes to protect them against the wind, and their long roots also help to anchor them. Look for butterflies, too.
Don't try to climb steep cliffs!

Salt Marshes

Sea Aster

Thrift

Salt marsh plants are unusual because they are regularly covered by the tide. Look out,

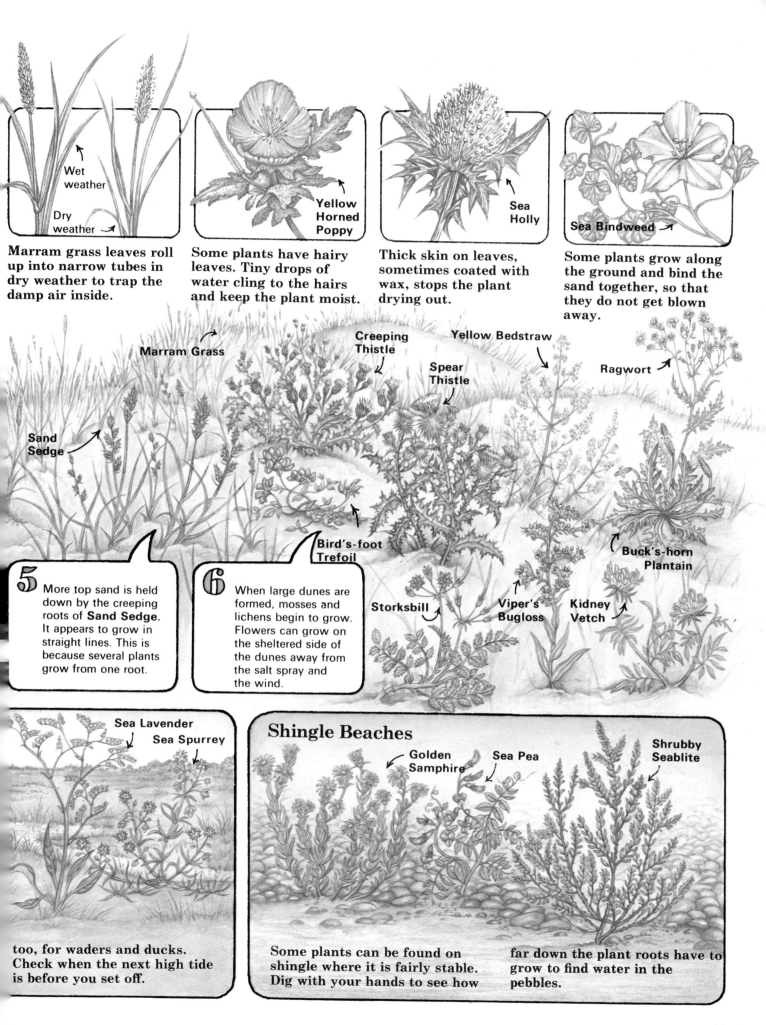

Wet weather

Dry weather

Yellow Horned Poppy

Sea Holly

Sea Bindweed

Marram grass leaves roll up into narrow tubes in dry weather to trap the damp air inside.

Some plants have hairy leaves. Tiny drops of water cling to the hairs and keep the plant moist.

Thick skin on leaves, sometimes coated with wax, stops the plant drying out.

Some plants grow along the ground and bind the sand together, so that they do not get blown away.

Marram Grass

Creeping Thistle

Yellow Bedstraw

Spear Thistle

Ragwort

Sand Sedge

Bird's-foot Trefoil

Buck's-horn Plantain

5 More top sand is held down by the creeping roots of **Sand Sedge**. It appears to grow in straight lines. This is because several plants grow from one root.

6 When large dunes are formed, mosses and lichens begin to grow. Flowers can grow on the sheltered side of the dunes away from the salt spray and the wind.

Storksbill

Viper's Bugloss

Kidney Vetch

Sea Lavender

Sea Spurrey

too, for waders and ducks. Check when the next high tide is before you set off.

Shingle Beaches

Golden Samphire

Sea Pea

Shrubby Seablite

Some plants can be found on shingle where it is fairly stable. Dig with your hands to see how far down the plant roots have to grow to find water in the pebbles.

13

Collecting Shells

The empty shells you find on the beach once belonged to molluscs—soft-bodied animals without internal skeletons. Some molluscs live on the shore. Others live in the sea, but you may find their shells washed up on the shore. To identify your shell, you must first decide which group of molluscs it belongs to. Some will be gastropods, which have a single, usually coiled shell, like Whelks and Periwinkles.

Check whether your gastropod shell coils clockwise or anti-clockwise as you look down on its pointed top.

Bivalves are molluscs with two (bi) shells (or valves), held together by muscles. Empty bivalve shells often break apart in the sea, but if you find both halves together, see if they are the same shape and size, as in Mussels, or unequal, as in Scallops.

Shapes and Colours

Shell colours show up best when the shells are wet. Some shells vary in colour. You could make a collection of shells of the same kind with different colours. The shape of shells can vary, too, depending on where they live.

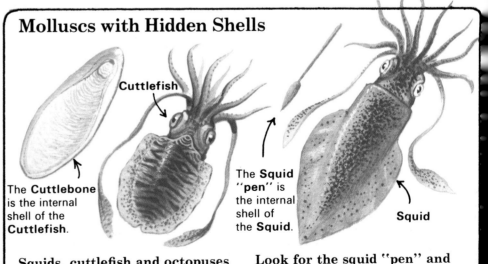

Look for **Flat Periwinkles** on Bladder or Knotted Wrack. They can be yellow, brown, orange or striped.

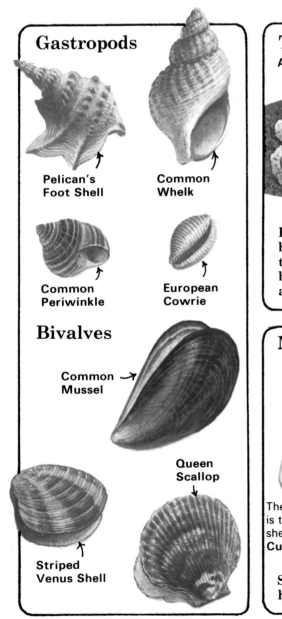

Gastropods

Pelican's Foot Shell

Common Whelk

Common Periwinkle

European Cowrie

Bivalves

Common Mussel

Queen Scallop

Striped Venus Shell

These are not Molluscs

Acorn Barnacles

Barnacles stick to rocks and build a hard wall round themselves, like a shell. They belong to the same group of animals as crabs.

Molluscs with Hidden Shells

Cuttlefish

The **Cuttlebone** is the internal shell of the **Cuttlefish**.

The **Squid** "pen" is the internal shell of the **Squid**.

Squid

Squids, cuttlefish and octopuses have a shell inside their bodies.

Look for the squid "pen" and cuttlebone on the shore.

Limpet shells on exposed rock faces are low and broad, to resist the sea.

Limpet shells hidden in crevices are taller and narrower. They are protected by the rock.

Painted Top Shells can be yellow or pink with red streaks, or white.

Pullet Carpet Shells vary in size. The smaller ones live on Mediterranean coasts.

Shells with Holes

Some molluscs poke tubes through the holes in their shell for sucking in water.

Hole made by an **Oyster Drill**

Keyhole Limpet

Ormer

Oyster

Holes in shells are either used for sucking in water, or are made by molluscs that drill holes in the shells of other molluscs. The Oyster Drill feeds on Oysters in this way.

1 How to Collect Shells

Thick paper for labels

Magnifying glass

Pen

Plastic bags

Bucket

Trowel

Take these things with you. Search low down on the shore, on rocks, under seaweed and stones, in pools and in the sand.

2

Label

Put each shell in a separate bag, with a label saying where you found it.

3

Newspaper →

Warm water

When you get home, clean your shells in warm water with a soft brush. Leave them to dry on newspaper.

4

Varnish

Shoe box

Cotton wool

Sticky label

Brush a thin coat of varnish on each shell. Keep your collection *either* in a shoe box lined with cotton wool . . .

5

Glue

Sticky label

Glue

Glue

Beads

. . . *or* make a chest of drawers by sticking together several large matchboxes. Label the fronts and sew on beads for handles.

Looking at Shells

This picture shows where molluscs live, how they feed, how they fix themselves to rocks so they are not washed away by the sea, and how some can live both in and out of the water. Some gastropods eat seaweed. They file off bits of the plant with their rough "tongue". Others use the "tongue" to drill a hole in the shells of other molluscs, and scrape off bits of the animal inside. Most bivalves suck in sea water and feed off the tiny plants and animals in it.

Follow the Limpet

Mark some Limpets and the rock next to them with quick-drying paint. When you go back in a few hours, you will be able to see how far they have moved.

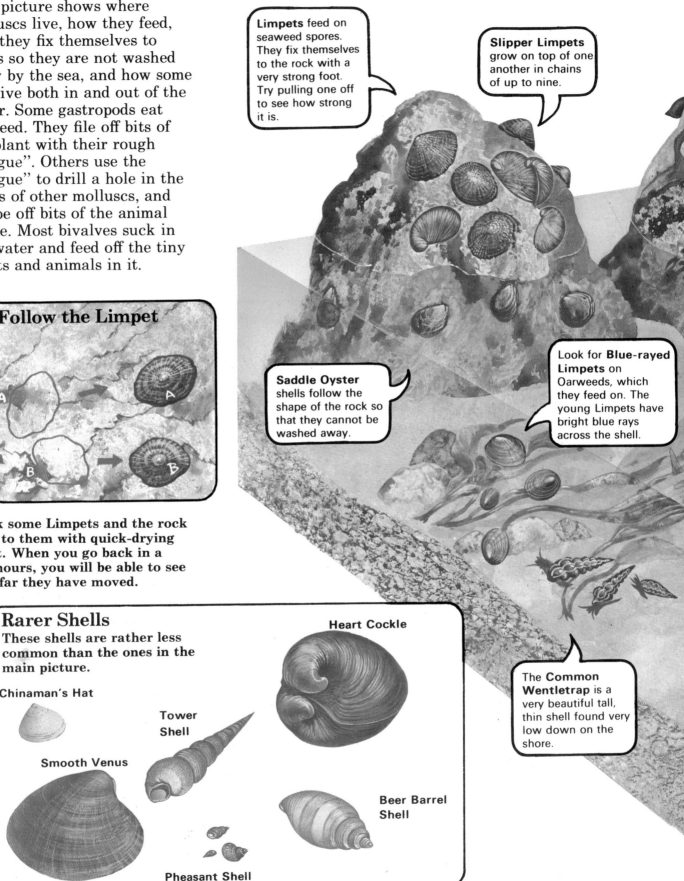

Limpets feed on seaweed spores. They fix themselves to the rock with a very strong foot. Try pulling one off to see how strong it is.

Slipper Limpets grow on top of one another in chains of up to nine.

Saddle Oyster shells follow the shape of the rock so that they cannot be washed away.

Look for **Blue-rayed Limpets** on Oarweeds, which they feed on. The young Limpets have bright blue rays across the shell.

The **Common Wentletrap** is a very beautiful tall, thin shell found very low down on the shore.

Rarer Shells

These shells are rather less common than the ones in the main picture.

Chinaman's Hat

Smooth Venus

Tower Shell

Heart Cockle

Pheasant Shell

Beer Barrel Shell

Common Periwinkles come off the rocks easily, but the rounded shape of their shell prevents them being smashed by the waves.

The **Rough Periwinkle** hides in cracks. When the tide is out, Periwinkles stick their shells to the rock, trapping a little water inside to keep them damp.

Piddocks are bivalves with rows of spines on their shells. They bore into rocks for protection.

Dog Whelks that feed on Mussels, their favourite food, become dark-coloured. Those that feed on Barnacles become white.

Mussels attach themselves to rocks by thin brown threads, to resist the beating of the waves.

Hermit Crabs have no shell of their own. Instead they live in empty gastropod shells, moving to a bigger shell as they grow.

Edible Cockles are bivalves that live in the sand. They have tubes, rather like small vacuum cleaners, for feeding on tiny bits of dead animals and plants lying on the sand.

Thin Tellins live in the sand and feed through siphons which they push above the surface. The siphons filter plankton from the sea water.

Look for small yellow and pink **Banded Chink Shells** on seaweed well down on the lower shore.

Look in muddy gravel for the **Baltic Tellin.** Like all Tellins, it has very long siphons for feeding off the surface of the sea bottom.

REMEMBER! PUT LIVE SHELLS BACK – THE RIGHT WAY UP – AS QUICKLY AS POSSIBLE, OTHERWISE YOU MIGHT KILL THEM. ONLY COLLECT EMPTY SHELLS

17

Watching Cliff Birds

How Seabirds Soar

Wind

Wind from the sea is pushed up as it hits cliffs. Seabirds "soar" in these up-currents of air, almost without moving their wings.

The **Kittiwake** has shorter legs than other gulls. Note the triangular black wing tips and black legs.

Ravens glide, dive and can even turn upside down. They eat shellfish, grain and small animals.

Herring Gulls nest in colonies. They nest on cliff ledges, on the ground, and even on buildings.

Cormorants can often be seen standing with their wings spread out. They sometimes fly many miles inland.

The **Great Black-backed Gull** is a very large gull, with a wing span of 1.5 m. It is very fierce, and sometimes kills and eats other seabirds.

Puffins nest in soft parts of the cliff. They use their large bills for burrowing and fighting. In winter the bill loses its brightly coloured outer layer.

Gannets build large nests (up to 60 cm. high) of seaweed, feathers, grass and earth. This is a chick.

The **Razorbill** has a stout body with short wings. It flies fast and swims well.

Manx Shearwaters almost touch the water as they glide over the sea. They are easy to recognize as they are black on top, white underneath.

Guillemots dive from the surface to catch fish. They can stay under water for up to a minute.

Gannets dive 30 m. or more to catch fish, which they swallow whole. Note the black wing tips, snowy white plumage, and strong flight with regular wing beats.

The **Storm Petrel**, our smallest seabird, flutters over the water looking for plankton and small fish. Note the square-shaped tail.

The **Fulmar** is fatter and fluffier than gulls. It glides on stiff wings, using the wind currents along the cliff face.

The **Shag** is very like the Cormorant, but it is smaller and thinner. It has a fast, direct flight, and often perches on rocks.

REMEMBER! DON'T GO NEAR THE CLIFF EDGE OR TRY TO CLIMB CLIFFS NEVER TAKE BIRDS' EGGS OR DISTURB THEIR NESTING PLACES

The **Kittiwake**, a small gull, makes a nest of green seaweed stuck to the cliff with mud.

Razorbills nest in colonies, laying their single egg in a crevice or under a boulder on the cliff.

Guillemots lay a single egg on bare rock. The egg is pear-shaped, so it rolls round instead of falling off the cliff.

All these birds nest on cliffs or rocky islands. Some nest in groups, called colonies, which you may be able to visit. But even if you cannot get very close to the birds, it is still interesting to watch them in flight, and possible to identify many of them.

19

Birds on the Beach

Salt marshes and muddy shores are good places to look for waders, ducks and geese. Look for waders, gulls, and terns on sandy beaches. Some of these birds migrate from the far north in winter to find better feeding places. Notice especially how the birds you see move on the ground, and how they feed, to help you to identify them. Remember that many birds change their plumage in winter, often becoming duller in colour.

1 Keeping Safe

Little Tern's egg

Birds that nest on the shore have eggs that are patterned to blend in with the sand or stones where they are laid.

2

Redshank on nest

Some birds build nests that blend in with the background to hide them from enemies. The Redshank builds its nest with grass in a tuft of grass.

The **Herring Gull** drops shells from the air onto rocks to burst them open.

The **Sanderling** darts along the tide line looking for shrimps, molluscs and worms.

Black-headed Gulls paddle in wet sand to bring animals to the surface.

The **Common Tern** dives to catch small fish, especially Sand-Eels.

The **Redshank** probes in the sand for worms and small molluscs.

A baby **Herring Gull** will beg for food by pecking at a red spot on the parent's bill.

Turnstones use their short sharp bills to find animals under stones and seaweed.

The male **Little Tern**, like other terns, gives Sand-Eels to the female in the courtship ceremony.

The **Bar-tailed Godwit** probes wet mud for insects and molluscs to eat.

The **Oystercatcher** uses its bill to dislodge Limpets and prise open Mussels to eat.

3

Ringed Plover dragging its wing

Some birds pretend to be hurt if their eggs or chicks are in danger. The enemy then follows the parent bird, instead of attacking the nest.

Danger from Oil

Cormorant

When birds get covered in oil emptied into the sea from tankers, they cannot fly or swim, and many starve to death or swallow the oil when preening, and poison themselves. The oil mats the bird's feathers together. Then the bird can no longer keep a layer of warm air under its feathers, so many die of cold.

Sometimes, however, they can be saved. If you find a live bird coated in oil, contact the local RSPCA clinic. Do not try to clean the bird yourself.

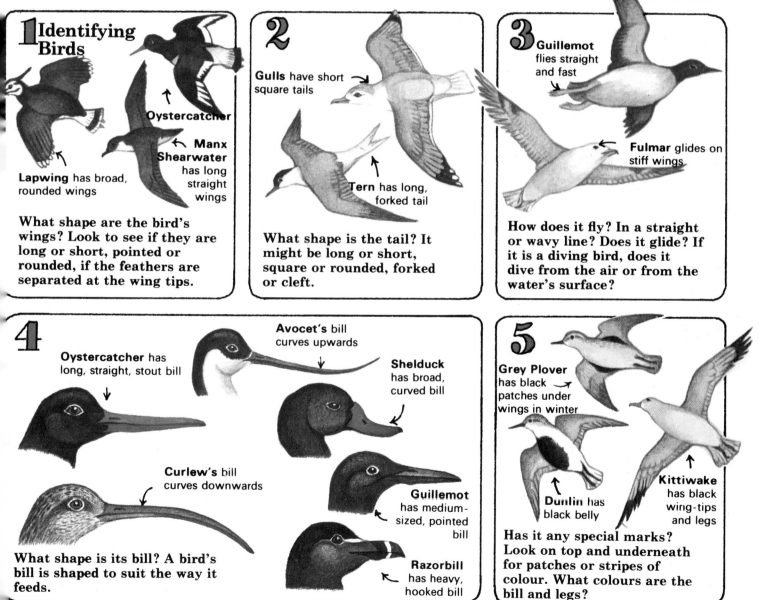

1 Identifying Birds

Oystercatcher

Manx Shearwater has long straight wings

Lapwing has broad, rounded wings

What shape are the bird's wings? Look to see if they are long or short, pointed or rounded, if the feathers are separated at the wing tips.

2

Gulls have short square tails

Tern has long, forked tail

What shape is the tail? It might be long or short, square or rounded, forked or cleft.

3

Guillemot flies straight and fast

Fulmar glides on stiff wings

How does it fly? In a straight or wavy line? Does it glide? If it is a diving bird, does it dive from the air or from the water's surface?

4

Oystercatcher has long, straight, stout bill

Avocet's bill curves upwards

Shelduck has broad, curved bill

Curlew's bill curves downwards

Guillemot has medium-sized, pointed bill

Razorbill has heavy, hooked bill

What shape is its bill? A bird's bill is shaped to suit the way it feeds.

5

Grey Plover has black patches under wings in winter

Dunlin has black belly

Kittiwake has black wing-tips and legs

Has it any special marks? Look on top and underneath for patches or stripes of colour. What colours are the bill and legs?

Animal Life in the Sand and Mud

At first sight a sandy beach may look empty. But if you dig down you can find many animals that burrow, especially on sheltered beaches where the sand is stable. There are no clear zones in the sand, because the conditions stay the same in spite of the tides. The animals simply burrow deeper to find moisture when the tide is out. You will find more animals near the surface if you dig along the low tide mark.

Animals that Live in Mud

Blunt Gaper

Common Otter Shell

Peppery Furrow Shell

Mud shifts about less than sand, so the shells that live in it do not need to move about as much as sand-dwellers. This makes them easier to dig up.

Notice that some shells are strong and thick to withstand the weight of the mud.

The **Sand Mason** worm builds a tube of sand and bits of shell around itself.

Signs on the Sand

Look out for clues on the surface of the sand that give away the hiding places of burrowing animals. You will have to dig down fast to catch up with them.

Empty **Actaeon** shells mean live ones are probably buried in the sand beneath.

Lugworm hollows and casts show where the two ends of the worm's burrow are.

The **Sea Potato** is a heart urchin. Look out for the dent it leaves above its burrow.

Lugworm in U-shaped burrow

The **Netted Whelk** is one of the few gastropods that lives in the sand. Look out for its feeding siphon sticking up as it ploughs along the surface. Note the ribs on its shell that give it its name.

Most **bivalves** live in the sand. You may see them disappearing as you approach. They often live in large groups. Some have ribbed shells to anchor them in the sand.

The **Masked Crab** lives in sand in the lower zone. It has a mask-like pattern on its shell.

The **Lesser Sand-Eel** is a common shore fish. Find it buried in sand in bays during spring and summer.

The **Sea Cucumber** is an animal, not a plant. This one can grow up to 30 cm. long.

Lesser Weever Fish →

A Burrowing Starfish

1   2

This starfish lives in the shallow water zone in the sand, but you may find it cast ashore (1) or see the mark it leaves as it burrows (2).

Look Under Heart Urchins

Close-up of Heart Urchin ↙

Tiny bivalves ↗

Look on the bottom of heart urchins among the spines for tiny bivalves that live there. Handle urchins gently as their spines rub off easily.

How Razor Shells Burrow

1 2 3 4

A Razor Shell has a "foot" which it pushes out of one end of its shell. It can dig very fast by contracting and expanding this foot. First it pulls itself upright (1, 2) then pushes the foot into the sand and pulls itself down (3, 4).

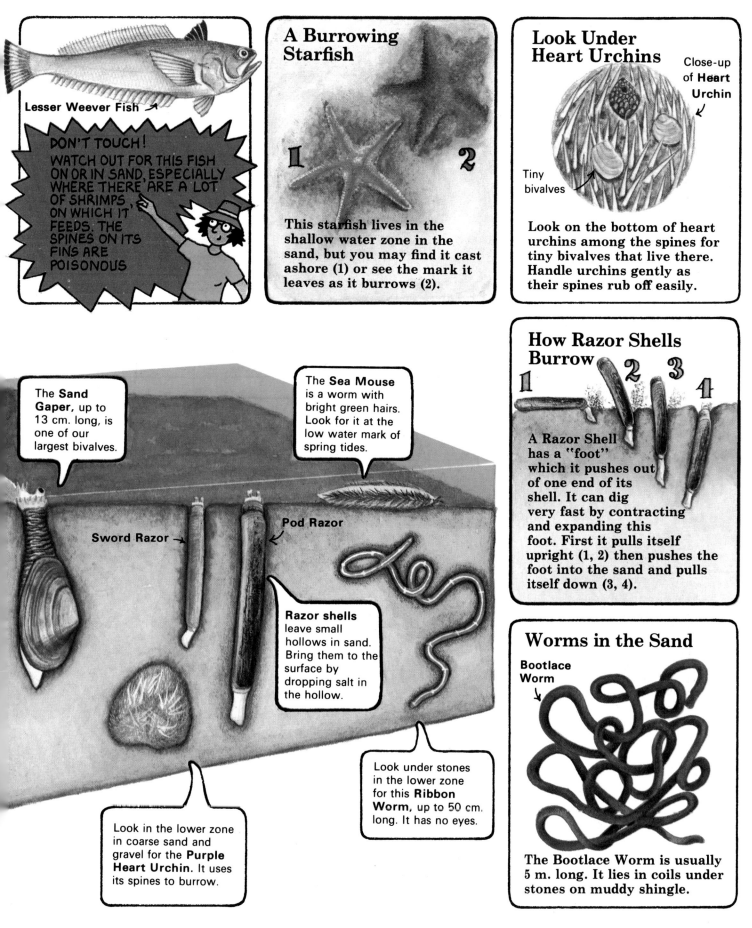

The **Sand Gaper**, up to 13 cm. long, is one of our largest bivalves.

The **Sea Mouse** is a worm with bright green hairs. Look for it at the low water mark of spring tides.

Sword Razor →

Pod Razor ↙

Razor shells leave small hollows in sand. Bring them to the surface by dropping salt in the hollow.

Look in the lower zone in coarse sand and gravel for the **Purple Heart Urchin**. It uses its spines to burrow.

Look under stones in the lower zone for this **Ribbon Worm**, up to 50 cm. long. It has no eyes.

Worms in the Sand

Bootlace Worm ↓

The Bootlace Worm is usually 5 m. long. It lies in coils under stones on muddy shingle.

Fishes

Some kinds of fish are more difficult to identify than others because their colours vary between the male and female, and between adults and young. Look for fish in pools, estuaries, and shallow water in bays. Remember that some, like eels, spend part of their life in the sea and part in fresh water. Some fish feed on seaweed and plankton, others on worms, molluscs and other fish.

Flat Fish

Look in the shallow water zone for these flat fish. You will only find small specimens —the larger ones live in deep water. Notice how their colours act as a camouflage. They hide by flapping their fins on the sea bottom to cover themselves with sand.

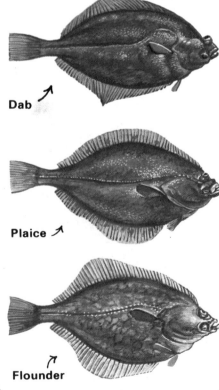

Dab ↗

Plaice ↗

Flounder ↗

The **Lumpsucker** has a large, strong sucker on its underside for fixing itself to rocks. It has no scales, but notice the rows of lumps, called tubercles, on its body.

The **Spotted Goby** swims in shoals among seaweed just below low tide mark, and in harbours.

Lesser Sand-Eels swim in large shoals over sand. Their silvery colour makes them hard to see.

Look in weedy rock pools for the **15-Spined Stickleback**. In spring the male builds, guards and cleans its nest.

The **Grey Gurnard** lives on the seabed. It probes the bottom with feelers to find worms and crustaceans to eat.

The **Tompot Blenny** is found low down on rocky shores. It grows to about 30 cm. long.

Montagu's **Sea Snail** has a sucker, but no scales or tubercles. Look under seaweed. It lays its eggs on Oarweed holdfasts and rocks.

The **Butterfish (or Gunnel)** is a relative of the Blenny. It has a flat body and rounded tail, and a very slippery skin. It lives under rocks.

The **Sand** or **Common Goby** is patterned like the sand. Notice the dark spot on its dorsal fin. Gobies have a fin underneath which forms a weak sucker.

Conger Eels, up to 2 m. long, hide in cracks and under stones in the lower zone of rocky shores. They come out at night to feed. Beware of their sharp teeth!

Look in eelgrass very low down on the shore for the **Greater Pipe-Fish**. It has a long snout.

Look under seaweed in small pools for the **Long-Spined Sea Scorpion**. Its spines are sharp, but not poisonous.

The **Cornish Sucker** hides under stones. It has a strong sucker on its underside.

The **Corkwing Wrasse** hides in crevices. Wrasses are very colourful, heavily-built fish with thick lips and strong teeth.

Beachcombing

Above or on the high water level, you will see a line of dead seaweed and rubbish thrown up by the sea onto the beach. This is called the strand line. If you look more closely, you may find some interesting things, some alive, others dead. It is also a good place to look for animals and birds that find their food among this rubbish, like Sandhoppers, beetles, flies, gulls and Turnstones.

Some beachcombers hunt along the strand line for shipping objects, like cork and glass floats, old bottles, and fishing nets.

Things that Look like Stones

Ammonite

Belemnite

This is the fossil of an animal related to squids and octopuses.

Bean

This coiled fossil is the remains of an animal that lived millions of years ago. It shows the shape of the animal's shell.

This bean-shaped object is the fruit of a West Indian plant, up to 5 cm. across.

Look in the lower zone on Eel Grass for rows of flat **egg cases of Netted Dog Whelks**.

Egg cases on little stalks belong to the **Common Dog Whelk**. Look in rock crevices.

A relative of the jellyfish, the **Portuguese Man-o'-War** may be cast ashore. Do not touch! This animal can sting.

Aurelia aurita is a very common jellyfish.

Crab shell

Egg cases of Netted Dog Whelk

Crab shell

Egg case of a Ray. These, and the cases of Dogfish, are called "mermaid's purses".

Dogfish egg cases have long tendrils. They will probably be empty.

Look for **empty crab shells**. As crabs get bigger, they shed their shells and grow a skin, which hardens to form a new shell.

Dead Animals

Fish tag

Bird rings and tags

Bird ring

Seal tag

Animals are ringed so that their movements can be traced. If you find any of these animals dead on the beach, look for a ring or tag. Send any that you find to the address on the tag, with a note of where and when you found it. Send bird rings to the address given on page 32.

REMEMBER — NEVER EAT ANYTHING YOU FIND ON THE BEACH, DEAD OR ALIVE. WATCH OUT FOR BROKEN GLASS AND OIL. YOU CAN CLEAN OIL OFF YOUR FEET WITH EUCALYPTUS OIL AND COTTON WOOL

If you find small holes in driftwood, try cutting off strips with a penknife to find **Shipworms** in their burrows.

Look on driftwood for the stalked **Goose Barnacles**.

Hornwrack becomes brittle and turns from brown to yellow when cast ashore.

A small group of molluscs has **tusk-shaped shells**. You may find empty ones.

Gribble holes

This spongy yellow ball is a mass of **egg cases of the Common Whelk**.

Look inside Whelk egg cases for a **Long-Clawed Porcelain Crab**.

The **Gribble** makes tiny holes in wood. Cut into driftwood to find its tunnel near the surface.

Tiny **Sandhoppers** jump about on rotting seaweed. They also feed on it.

You may find **bones or skeletons** of birds and fish. You could clean them and make a collection.

27

More Seashore Life to Spot

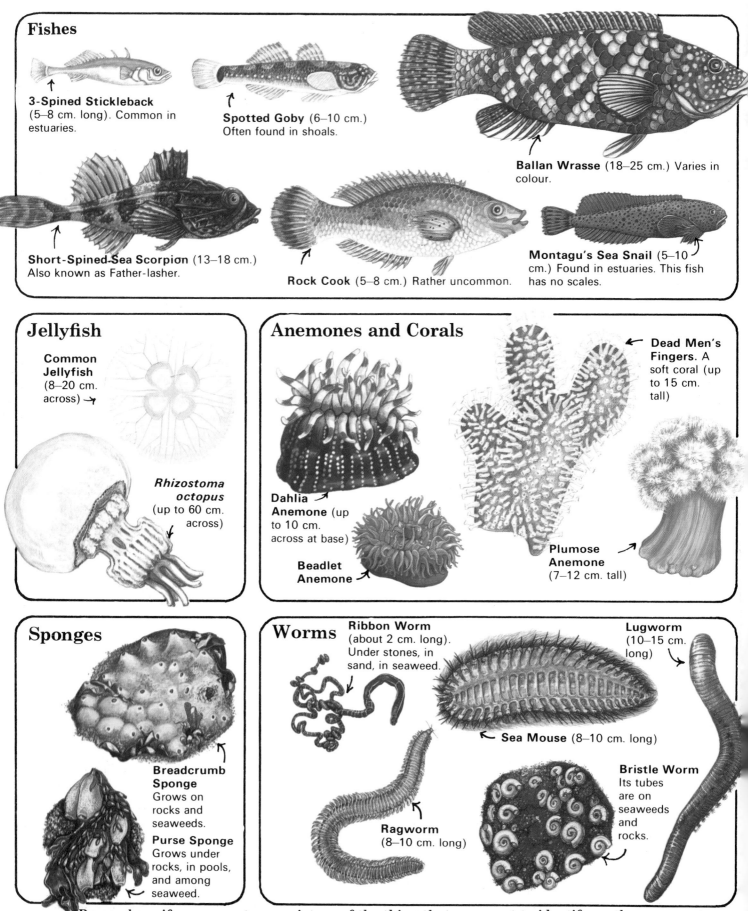

Fishes

3-Spined Stickleback (5–8 cm. long). Common in estuaries.

Spotted Goby (6–10 cm.) Often found in shoals.

Ballan Wrasse (18–25 cm.) Varies in colour.

Short-Spined Sea Scorpion (13–18 cm.) Also known as Father-lasher.

Rock Cook (5–8 cm.) Rather uncommon.

Montagu's Sea Snail (5–10 cm.) Found in estuaries. This fish has no scales.

Jellyfish

Common Jellyfish (8–20 cm. across)

Rhizostoma octopus (up to 60 cm. across)

Anemones and Corals

Dead Men's Fingers. A soft coral (up to 15 cm. tall)

Dahlia Anemone (up to 10 cm. across at base)

Beadlet Anemone

Plumose Anemone (7–12 cm. tall)

Sponges

Breadcrumb Sponge Grows on rocks and seaweeds.

Purse Sponge Grows under rocks, in pools, and among seaweed.

Worms

Ribbon Worm (about 2 cm. long). Under stones, in sand, in seaweed.

Lugworm (10–15 cm. long)

Sea Mouse (8–10 cm. long)

Ragworm (8–10 cm. long)

Bristle Worm Its tubes are on seaweeds and rocks.

Remember—if you cannot see a picture of the thing that you want to identify on these pages, turn to the page earlier in the book that deals with that kind of animal or plant.

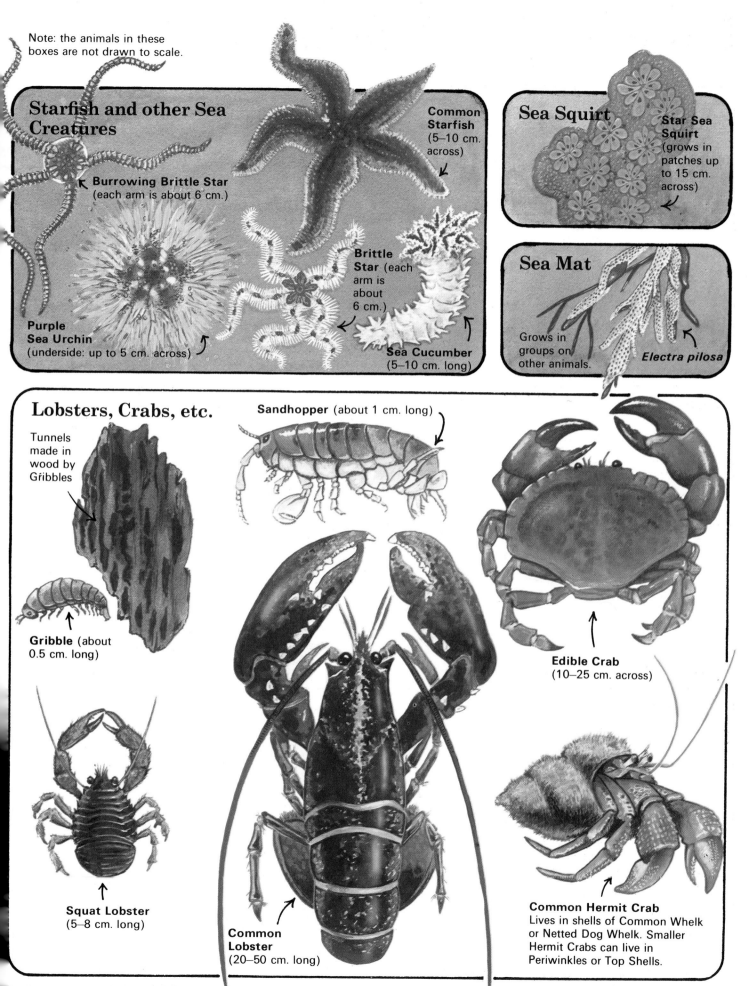

Note: the animals in these boxes are not drawn to scale.

Starfish and other Sea Creatures

Burrowing Brittle Star (each arm is about 6 cm.)

Common Starfish (5–10 cm. across)

Brittle Star (each arm is about 6 cm.)

Purple Sea Urchin (underside: up to 5 cm. across)

Sea Cucumber (5–10 cm. long)

Sea Squirt

Star Sea Squirt (grows in patches up to 15 cm. across)

Sea Mat

Grows in groups on other animals.

Electra pilosa

Lobsters, Crabs, etc.

Sandhopper (about 1 cm. long)

Tunnels made in wood by Gribbles

Gribble (about 0.5 cm. long)

Edible Crab (10–25 cm. across)

Squat Lobster (5–8 cm. long)

Common Lobster (20–50 cm. long)

Common Hermit Crab
Lives in shells of Common Whelk or Netted Dog Whelk. Smaller Hermit Crabs can live in Periwinkles or Top Shells.

Remember—if you cannot see a picture of the thing that you want to identify on these pages, turn to the page earlier in the book that deals with that kind of animal or plant.

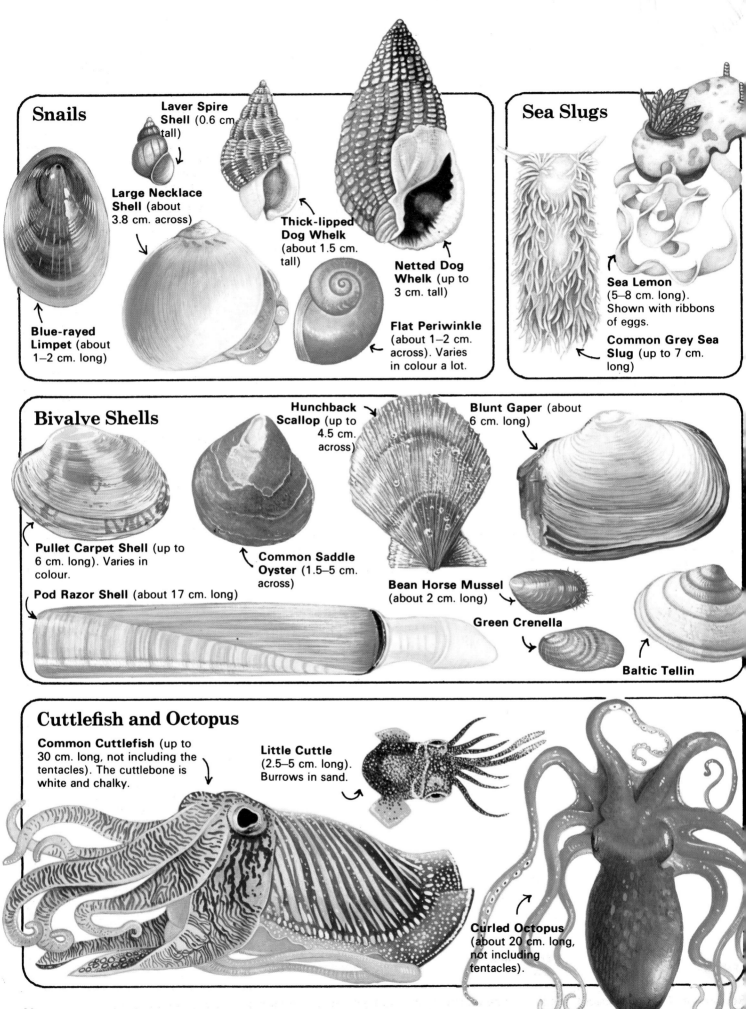

Snails

Laver Spire Shell (0.6 cm. tall)

Large Necklace Shell (about 3.8 cm. across)

Thick-lipped Dog Whelk (about 1.5 cm. tall)

Netted Dog Whelk (up to 3 cm. tall)

Flat Periwinkle (about 1–2 cm. across). Varies in colour a lot.

Blue-rayed Limpet (about 1–2 cm. long)

Sea Slugs

Sea Lemon (5–8 cm. long). Shown with ribbons of eggs.

Common Grey Sea Slug (up to 7 cm. long)

Bivalve Shells

Hunchback Scallop (up to 4.5 cm. across)

Blunt Gaper (about 6 cm. long)

Pullet Carpet Shell (up to 6 cm. long). Varies in colour.

Common Saddle Oyster (1.5–5 cm. across)

Pod Razor Shell (about 17 cm. long)

Bean Horse Mussel (about 2 cm. long)

Green Crenella

Baltic Tellin

Cuttlefish and Octopus

Common Cuttlefish (up to 30 cm. long, not including the tentacles). The cuttlebone is white and chalky.

Little Cuttle (2.5–5 cm. long). Burrows in sand.

Curled Octopus (about 20 cm. long, not including tentacles).

Birds

Fulmar. Nests on cliffs in summer.

Shelduck

Scaup Estuaries and bays in winter.

Common Scoter

Male   Female

Eider Duck Rocky and sandy sea coasts.

Knot. Has grey plumage in winter.

Sanderling. Has pale plumage in winter.

Grey Plover. Has greyer appearance in winter.

Oyster-catcher Shores, islands, estuaries.

Curlew Sand dunes and grassy coasts.

Greenshank Marshes, estuaries, and mud flats.

Lesser Black-Backed Gull. Coasts and estuaries. Nests on cliffs.

Male

Stonechat Sea cliffs

Female

Wheatear

Plants

Horned Wrack

Sea Lace

Edible Dulse

Furbelows

Cord Grass

Eel Grass

Lomentaria Clavellosa

Codium tomentosum

Gutlava

Remember—if you cannot see a picture of the thing that you want to identify on these pages, turn to the page earlier in the book that deals with that kind of animal or plant.

Index

Books to Read

Collins Pocket Guide to the Sea Shore. J. Barret and C. M. Yonge (Collins)
The Seashore. C. M. Yonge (Collins)
The Observer's Book of Sea and Seashore. ed. I. O. Evans (Warne)
Seashore Life in Colour. Gwynne Vevers (Blandford)
Seashore Ecology. P. M. Miles and H. B. Miles (Hulton Educational)
Seashore. Ian Murray (Black)
Exploring the Seashore. Leslie Jackman (Evans)
The Shell Book of Beachcombing. Tony Soper (David and Charles)
The Birds of Britain and Europe. Heinzel, Fitter and Parslow (Collins)

Clubs to Join

The Council for Environmental Conservation (address: Zoological Gardens, Regent's Park, London NW1) will supply the addresses of your local **Natural History Societies.** (Send a stamped self-addressed envelope for the list.) Many of these have specialist sections and almost all have field meetings. **The Royal Society for Nature Conservation** (address: 22 The Green, Nettleham, Lincoln) will give you the address of your local **County Naturalist Trust,** which may have a junior branch. Many of the Trusts have meetings and lectures and offer opportunities for work on nature reserves.

For birdwatching, the national club is the **Young Ornithologists' Club,** The Lodge, Sandy, Bedfordshire. SG19 2DL.
Other useful addresses:
The Countryside Commission, John Dower House, Crescent Place, Cheltenham, Gloucestershire.
The Nature Conservancy Council, 19/20 Belgrave Square, London SW1X 8PY.
The British Trust for Ornithology, Beech Grove, Station Road, Tring, Herts. (Send **bird rings** to them).